WINGS No. 2

US Nav
West Coast W

George Hall
with Dan Bayer and Chad Slattery

Windrow & Greene

© 1992 Windrow & Greene Ltd.

Published in Great Britain by
Windrow & Greene Ltd.
5 Gerrard Street
London W1V 7LJ

Published in the USA by
Specialty Press Publishers &
Wholesalers Inc.
P.O. Box 338
Stillwater, MN 55082
(612) 430-2210/800-888-9653

A CIP catalogue record for this book
is available from the British Library

ISBN-1-872004-32-6

(Title page) If Hugh Heffner could
afford his own air force he would
probably include a Tomcat or two
within its ranks; but he would have to
sell a few million more copies per
month to be able to afford the
running costs of this flash feline.
Flagship of Air Test and Evaluation
Squadron Four (VX-4), this F-14A-90-
GR (BuNo 159853) wore the
traditional glossy black scheme
pioneered by the unit's F-4J Phantom
II BuNo 153783, christened *Vandy
One*, in the early 1970s. The Tomcat
received its one-off paint job in the
winter of 1989, just in time to take
over from the last all-black Phantom
II on strength with VX-4. F-4S BuNo
158360 was retired from squadron
service in the spring of 1990, ending
the Navy's operational use of the
venerable Phantom II.

The thick coastal sea fog
thousands of feet below provides
this PMTC F-14A with the perfect
canvas on which to display the
effectiveness of its tactical paint
scheme (TPS). Only the old style
gloss gull grey external tanks and the
AIM-54 missile pallets break up the
overall camouflage, although the
smart black fin trim clearly advertises
the aircraft's owners.

New, more reliable versions of the
AIM-7 Sparrow have also entered
service since the Tomcat's initial
missile trials, the viability of both the
Lima and Mike models of this
venerable medium-range weapon
being tested at Point Mugu. Finally,
the fighter pilot's favourite missile —
the AIM-9 Sidewinder — has also
matured since the early 1970s, the all-
aspect Lima and Mike rounds
replacing the earlier G-,J- and H-
models in fleet ranks. All these
versions have been exhaustively
tested by the PMTC and VX-4 before

West Coast Warriors

being released to frontline squadrons. Currently the AIM-9R solid-state Sidewinder, with electro-optical seeker operating in both visual and infrared wavelengths, is being put through its paces; as is the Sparrow replacement, the AIM-120 AMRAAM (Advanced Medium-Range Air-to-Air Missile).

These weapons will provide the 'bite' for the newer versions of the venerable Tomcat well into the 21st century.

As far as the aircraft itself is concerned, the interim Bravo and the more definitive Delta model have both been thoroughly wrung out in the clear Californian skies prior to service clearance. A pair of pre-production F-14Ds, for example,

spent two months in late 1990 at Point Mugu undergoing a full-scale Navy technical evaluation (TechEval) prior to the aircraft's release to VX-4 for operational testing. During the TechEval the aircrew (from both Point Mugu and the Naval Air Test Center at Patuxent River) logged more than 130 sorties and 300 hours on the Tomcats, the aircraft being maintained in a 'total force' effort by both Navy and Grumman personnel. This two-phase exercise initially saw the Tomcats based at Pax River in Maryland, testing the aircraft's radar and ECCM abilities.

When compared to other Naval Air Stations in California like Miramar and Lemoore, Point Mugu appears to lack the abundance of fighter and strike aircraft which jostle for ramp space at these bases. There are less than a dozen Tomcats scattered across the tarmac at Mugu, and the majority of the Hornets here wear the colours of the naval reserve unit VFA-305 'Lobos'. However, if it wasn't for this facility, located 40 miles due north of Los Angeles on the rugged California coast, the US Navy would be bereft of combat aircraft to equip its frontline fleet units. Moreover, none of the weapons systems which make the modern crop of fighter and strike aircraft so potent would be available for use.

Through the auspices of the Pacific Missile Test Center (PMTC) and specialist squadrons like VX-4 and -5, both aircraft types and weapons systems are thoroughly evaluated at Point Mugu before their release to fleet units. This testing involves the use of state-of-the-art equipment in purpose-built laboratories; current aircraft types; fully instrumented weapons ranges out over the Pacific; intelligent drones capable of simulating any target likely to be encountered; and live missile firings.

This specialized role has been Point Mugu's *raison d'etre* since the late 1940s. The first weapon tested at the base was the pulse-jet powered LOON missile, developed from the German V1 rocket. Since then, more missiles have been launched from Mugu than from any other major test range in the Western world. Although initially used exclusively by the Navy, the range was redesignated a national facility in 1958, opening it to the Air Force, Army, Marine Corps and NASA. The Sea Test Range comprises a fully instrumented 35,000 square mile area, which is roughly 125 miles wide and 250 miles long. All the Navy's major weapon systems — the AIM-7 Sparrow, AIM-9 Sidewinder, AIM-54 Phoenix, AGM-88 HARM, Harpoon and AIM-120 AMRAAM — have undergone development testing at Mugu, and update and enhancement programmes continue on many of these missiles today.

Aircraft such as the F-4 Phantom II, F-14 Tomcat and F/A-18 Hornet have all proven their respective manufacturers' performance claims in the skies over Mugu. New versions of the Navy's staple types have all been developed by Grumman, Lockheed and McDonnell Douglas with the test pilots' reports from Mugu firmly in mind. Currently, the F-14D and the Night Hornet are being put through their paces by VX-4 and -5, while older types like the baseline A-model Tomcat and Hornet are still being progressively updated with avionics and weapons fits tested at Mugu.

Reserve aviation is also a major player in the day-to-day operations of the Naval Air Station. No less than 1,800 reservists serve in 22 units located in and around the Mugu area. The three largest units based at the air station are VP-65 'Tridents', equipped with the P-3 Orion; VFA-305 'Lobos', who fly the F/A-18 Hornet; and

HCS-5 'Firehawks', who are tasked with performing strike rescue duties in their HH-60 Seahawks.

The mix of prototypes, test aircraft, missiles, drones and reserve assets ensures a full flight pattern over the base at all times. The role of test and evaluation will continue to play a crucial part in the base's routine, its electronic ranges being utilized well into the 21st century. The latest generation of fleet warplanes due on-line later in the 1990s also have a date in the skies over Mugu, as this remarkable facility continues to perform at the leading edge of technology in support of a new breed of 'West Coast warriors'.

Virtually head-on, and the pilot has the wings swept fully through to 20° leading-edge sweep to keep the Tomcat hanging in there close behind the C-130 Hercules photo–ship. Despite the Herk's modest cruising speed (200 to 250 knots) throughout the brief photographic sortie, the F–14 pilot never once had to resort to deploying the full–span leading edge slats to maintain stability while at the 'shallow end' of his flight envelope. Winking away beneath the bulbous nose of the aircraft is one of two anti–collision beacons fitted to the Tomcat, the second high intensity strobe being faired into the leading edge of the fin tip on the port vertical surface. Immediately above the nose light is the all-seeing Northrop AN/AXX-1 Television Camera Set (TCS), which can be used by the crew to visually identify targets at distances of up to nine miles or more, depending on weather conditions. The TCS is fully compatible with the F-14A's AWG-9 radar, and can display images of the radar's target on either the RIO's tactical information screen or the pilot's vertical display indicator. Beneath the beacon is a Sanders AN/ALQ-126 deception jamming transmitter, this device being automatically activated by the Tomcat's AN/APR-45 warning receivers when contact with enemy radar is achieved. Another '126 covering the rear hemisphere of the F-14 is mounted immediately above the port rudder in a small bullet fairing.

1: The Big Cat

The sea mist parts to reveal the deep blue expanse of the Pacific several thousand feet below. Aside from the glossy tanks and pallets, this Tomcat also wears an unusually coloured canopy fairing which is virginal in appearance. Typical squadron practice has the crew's names emblazoned on the long one-piece transparency rail on both sides, unlike the USAF policy which has the pilots name to port and the crew chief's to starboard. The cleanness of the hood suggests that this is a replacement part recently fitted to the aircraft.

The Grumman F-14 Tomcat is an ageless beast that looks as good now as it did 21 years ago. The fighter first took to the skies on 21 December 1970, Grumman chief test pilot Robert Smythe and project test pilot William 'Bob' Millar braving the wintry weather at Calverton to take the F-14 (BuNo 157980) aloft for two low-speed circuits of the airfield. Since that date, no fewer than 774 Tomcats have flown the same test circuit as the short-lived prototype (BuNo 157980 crashed on its second flight on 30 December 1970 due to massive hydraulic failure), these aircraft being issued to no less than 24 frontline and four reserve squadrons on both the East and West Coasts. However, before the mighty Tomcat could begin replacing the Phantom II in fleet service, the aircraft's revolutionary Hughes AN/AWG-9 radar and AIM-54 Phoenix long-range missile had to be fully integrated into the airframe, and shown to work satisfactorily against moving targets. This demanding task was given to the Pacific Missile Test Center (PMTC) at Naval Air Station (NAS) Point Mugu.

Of the initial pre-production run of 20 F-14s, four airframes were allocated to the PMTC, with one aircraft (the fifth prototype, BuNo 157984) being lost on 20 June 1973 after being struck by a dummy AIM-7E-2 Sparrow missile, which had pitched up seconds after being launched and ruptured an internal fuel tank, causing an uncontrollable fire. This freak accident was the only black spot during an intensive trials period with the Tomcat, the highlight of which was a six-Phoenix launch on 22 November 1973. Tasked with knocking down six drone targets flying at speeds between Mach 0.6 and 1.1 at ranges which varied from 31 to 50 nautical miles, the PMTC crew ripple-fired the AIM-54As over a period of 38 seconds while the Tomcat cruised at Mach 0.78 at a height of 28,400 feet. Although one missile went ballistic due to an antenna control loop failure, and another tracked a drone which strayed from its pre-programmed course (resulting in an unrealistic radar target), the remaining quartet of AIM-54s scored confirmed kills.

Further firings pitted the AWG-9/Phoenix pairing against Bomarc missiles and BQM-34 drones simulating MiG-25 *Foxbat* interceptors and Tupolev TU-22M *Backfire* bombers respectively. The *Foxbat* trials saw AIM-54s fired at Bomarcs flying at speeds in excess of Mach 2.7 at altitudes of 80,000 feet. To further enhance the Bomarc's MiG-25 simulation, the rounds were fitted with an augmentation system which made its radar-reflective area resemble that of a *Foxbat*. During the *Backfire* tests a drone fitted with a noise jammer was engaged at Mach 1.5 at 50,000 feet by a Phoenix launched from a Tomcat flying at Mach 1.5 at 44,000 feet. The missile travelled 110 nautical miles to achieve its kill, reaching a height of 103,500 feet during the mid-course of its flight.

The pace of the trials work barely let up with the Tomcat's clearance for fleet service, PMTC crews continuing to flesh out the aircraft's interception

parameters against both fighter threats and simulated Soviet anti-ship cruise missiles. Lessons learnt by the crews of the PMTC and VX-4 'Evaluators' were carefully annotated after every sortie; and at the end of the initial phase of testing in late 1973 the first Tactical Manuals for the F-14 were published for frontline units destined to take the Tomcat to sea.

Over the ensuing two decades, both units at Point Mugu have continued to test new weapons systems brought on-line for integration into the existing Tomcat package. Although the aircraft's appearance has remained essentially the same, new weapons have been developed for fleet use; the Phoenix, for example, has been developed from the baseline Alpha model through the interim Bravo version to today's potent AIM-54C.

For this sortie the PMTC armourers have bolted dummy AIM–54C and AIM-9M missiles onto the left shoulder pylon for guidance system evaluation. Although the weapons have been issued to fleet squadrons, development work continues on both systems. Flights will be performed to test newly improved software packages developed by the respective missiles' manufacturers, or perhaps to rectify an unusual technical glitch encountered on a weapon issued to a frontline unit. The mounting of Phoenix missiles on the wing pylons is rarely practised by fleet squadrons because of the drag penalties incurred by the bulky missile. When mounted along the centreline, flush with the aircraft's underside and hidden behind their specialized pallets, the AIM-54s cause few noticeable airflow problems; but when they are stuck out on exposed pylons the missiles' drag factor is soon reflected in the fuel gauge, reducing the crews' all-important CAP (Combat Air Patrol) loiter time out on station.

Simulated weapons firing was also practised using special 'golden bird' missiles, which allow crews to track and guide the round to a target just as if a weapon had been loosed off in combat; while various other sub-systems were put through their paces, including the Comm/Nav/IFF fit and the F-14D's compatibility with the TACTS and TARPS pods.

Phase II testing saw the aircraft operating from Point Mugu, using the base's offshore warning ranges, as well as the facilities at Edwards and Nellis. The emphasis was clearly placed on missile/aircraft operability while in California, the F-14D crews expending 12 missiles (five AIM-7M/Fs, five AIM-54Cs and two AIM-9Ls) during the course of the programme. Each mission scenario was tailored to test a specific aspect of the Delta's new Hughes APG-71 radar; multi-target, track-while-scan, long range and lookdown Sidewinder and Sparrow firings were all successfully completed against BQM-74 and -34 drones, Vandals and QF-86 Sabres. Even though the new F-14D is currently entering service with frontline units, and the venerable Alpha model is nearing its 20th anniversary with the fleet, testing and trials work on both versions still continues today. As long as the Tomcat darkens the cold steel aboard the Navy's carriers, the pilots and RIOs of the PMTC and VX-4 will, as a matter of daily routine, stride out onto the sun-bleached ramp at Point Mugu and strap into an F-14, be it an Alpha, Bravo or Delta model.

Tomcat for the 1990s: the revamped F-14D embodies both powerplant and avionics upgrades. The original Pratt & Whitney TF30 turbofans caused numerous headaches when the F-14A was initially issued to frontline units, fanblade separation and compressor stalls causing the loss of several aircraft in the first two years of service. Although the manufacturers quickly solved these faults, the

The distinctive PMTC crest has been worn on many varied types since the early 1950s, and has always symbolized excellence in the demanding field of test flying. Up until the mid-1980s, the stylized design was worn in full colour on the unit's Tomcats: but the 'low-vizzing' of the Navy's fighter fleet eventually took its toll on the Mugu-based units, and the crest was resprayed in matt black.

overall thrust produced by the TF30 (21,000 lbs st) was never impressive, pilots being forced to constantly 'fly' the engine in virtually all regimes. With the advent of the F-14D the TF30 has been replaced by the General Electric F110-GE-400, this engine producing 23,000 lbs st thrust in afterburner. Similar to the tried and proven engine used in the USAF's F-15 and F-16 fighters, the F110 gives the pilot unrestricted throttle control in any flight regime, as well as reducing the compressor stall problem which was synonymous with the TF30.

Up front, the Tomcat's prominent radome now contains the all-seeing Hughes AN/APG-71 radar, this digital system allowing the crew to launch Phoenix missiles at longer distances than those previously achieved with the analogue AWG-9. Capable of withstanding severe ECM interference, the APG-71 is a derivative of the APG-70 fitted in the F-15E Strike Eagle. Although both of these Tomcats are assigned to VX–4, only the lead fighter wears the unit's distinctive 'XF' codes on its twin fins. The gloss grey aircraft was one of the F-14Ds used by the PMTC during the TechEval conducted at Point Mugu in the autumn of 1990.

Possibly the most famous Tomcat of all, *Vandy One* of VX-4 was a smash-hit with airshow organisers up and down the West Coast. The aircraft was completely stripped of its standard drab grey scheme in late 1989 by the VX-4 paint shop, reappearing in this superb gloss black finish. Like the Phantom II before it, the F-14 was technically assigned to the most senior crew pairing Point Mugu could offer: the

base commanding officer up front, and the PMTC boss in back. In practice, the aircraft is utilized just like any other Tomcat in the VX-4 fleet, flying all manner of tasks and crewed by any of the squadron's experienced crop of pilots and RIOs. Unfortunately, *Vandy One* recently accrued enough hours to warrant a major airframe overhaul at NAS North Island in San Diego, being resprayed during rework and returned to VX-4 in TPS greys.

Zone Five, high-G 'bat turns' are a favourite of Tomcat crews on both coasts, and the VX-4 pilots maintain this tradition in the skies over Mugu at every available opportunity. Tight turns can be performed with the wings in sweepback or fully locked forward, the moving surfaces pivoting automatically in response to air data and altitude sensors mounted externally on the aircraft. The option of manual override is always available to the pilot. The wings themselves slot into a one-piece carry–through box constructed from electron-beam welded Ti-61A1-4V titanium alloy.

A fleet fighter by nature, the Tomcat's home is aboard the behemoth carriers of the US Navy, and in the course of testing the new F-14D VX-4 took to the high seas for an intense period of cyclic ops aboard USS *Nimitz* (CVN-68). Although most of the Delta's systems had already been evaluated at sea in the older Alpha and Bravo models, the complete package that is the F-14D still had to be cleared for blue water operations. Looking good for a three-wire, this Tomcat has short-, medium- and long-range missiles fitted to various weapons stations, as well as a pair of 267 US gal. external tanks beneath the engine intakes. A close examination of the under radome area reveals the distinctive twin-bullet fairings for the infrared search and track set (IRST) and the TCS, unique to the F-14D. Until the advent of this model earlier Tomcats carried either an IRST or a TCS system beneath the radome, but never both. As with the A- and B-models, the F-14D also carries an AN/ALQ-126 jammer scabbed to the underside of the twin pods.

Each fleet squadron has a small crop of very experienced aircrew who act as landing signals officers (LSOs) for their fellow pilots. Each landing is graded by the LSO, who is in constant radio contact with the pilot. When heading out to sea for any period of time, VX-4 embark at least two LSOs and a small team of maintainers to support the dedicated aircrew.

'Don't mess with me!' It is hard to imagine any pilot/aircraft combination that would relish stumbling across this VF-211 'Checkmates' F-14B — but then, the Phoenix/AWG-9 pairing would not allow hostile contact to get within 100 miles of the Tomcat unannounced. The six-pack Phoenix fit is rarely seen on the Tomcat, and although these missiles look impressive they are actually dummy rounds (as denoted by the blue circumference bands). Fleet squadrons only fly in this configuration when ashore at Oceana, or Miramar, as in this instance. When at sea, the Tomcat can launch with six AIM-54s but cannot recover with them still all aboard, as the aircraft's landing weight exceeds safety margins in the critical phase before embracing the arrestor wires.

Like the F-14D, the Bravo model is powered by a pair of GE F110s and has the modified gun gas dispersion vents over the M61A1 Vulcan cannon. Unlike the Delta, the interim Tomcat still retains the AWG-9 radar, and associated analogue displays in the cockpit.

VF-211 — along with Carrier Air Wing Nine (CVW-9) sister-squadron VF-24 'Renegades' — was the first fleet unit on the West Coast to re-equip with the F-14B, then designated the F-14A+, in early 1989. Only 69 F-14Bs have so far been issued to the fleet, 29 of which were new-build airframes while the remaining 40 were remanufactured F-14As. Recently the 'Checkmates' made F-14 history by becoming 'Bombcat' qualified, dropping inert 1000 lb Mk 83 iron bombs on range targets near MCAS Yuma, Arizona, on 8 August 1990. Along with VF-24, the 'Checkmates' proved that the F-14 could successfully operate in the strike/fighter role, the aircraft having originally been constructed by Grumman with the capability to carry up to 14,500 lbs of ordnance. Currently, only the Bravo and Delta models have the appropriate built-in computer software to enable the crew to deliver bombs and rockets successfully.

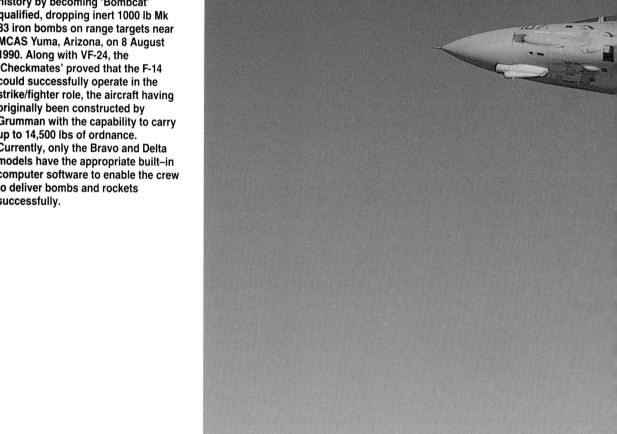

The first fleet unit to receive the F-14D was the West Coast training squadron VF-124 'Gunfighters', based at NAS Miramar. After working up on the 'new' Tomcat, the squadron's first task was to oversee the transition of VF-51 'Screaming Eagles' and VF-111 'Sundowners' from their baseline F-14As to the F-14D. This garish pairing, 'showboating' off Mugu, are both basic F-14As; the lion's share of the 'Gunfighter' fleet is made up of weary Alpha models. VF-124 have been in the business of training fighter crews for over 30 years, being established out of the redesignation

of VF-53 on 11 April 1958. At that time the F-8U Crusader was commencing service with the Navy, and VF-124 was issued with over 20 of the fighters to fulfil the Replacement Carrier Air Group duties for the Pacific fleet. Referred to as the 'Crusader College' throughout the 1960s, VF-124 trained thousands of naval aviators in the art of flying the F-8.

After 14 years of single-seat fighters, VF-124 eventually traded in its Crusaders for Tomcats in August 1972, thus becoming the first squadron in the Navy to receive the

Grumman jet in large numbers. After intense work-ups and the formulation of a training syllabus, the first trainee Tomcat crews commenced conversion onto the fighter with VF-124 in mid-1973, these pilots and RIOs going on to form the nucleus of the first fleet squadrons, VF-1 and -2. Almost 20 years later the 'Gunfighters' are still churning out new F-14 crews for fleet units, although the training syllabus has changed somewhat to reflect the arrival of the new, more effective, F-14D.

When compared to some of today's fourth generation fighters like the SU-27 *Flanker* and the F-16 Fighting Falcon, the Tomcat may look somewhat dated and a little asthmatic; but with the advent of the gutsy F-14D, with its state-of-the-art radar and healthier thrust-to-weight ratio, the sun is most definitely not setting on the undisputed 'king of the carrier deck'.

2: Hornet

(Previous page) Unlike the F-14, the Hornet has never been known for its interesting paint schemes and flamboyant unit markings, the aircraft ushering in a new era of drabness when introduced to fleet ranks back in 1983. Unfortunately Navy Reserve F/A-18s break little new ground when it comes to livening up the grey ramps at Mugu. Technically, all Navy and Marine Corps Hornets wear three separate shades of TPS grey overall, the shades becoming lighter the further you move down the fuselage. In reality, as can be seen on this weary 'Lobo', the Hornet wears one shade of medium grey overall, with a visibly darker colour being used for the anti-glare panel forward of the cockpit, the unit's distinctive emblem on the twin fins, and the star-and-bar and warning stencils strategically placed all over the airframe. Finally, black is used sparingly for the nose and fin tip modex, the unit designation, the pilot's name and, in this case, the unique wolf's head motif and the 'Battle E' excellence award. Although 'Lobo 413' is devoid of stores, heavy carbon deposits around the cannon port and gas purging intakes suggest that the pilot has been practising his markmanship on a splash target moored within Mugu's instrumented weapons range off the California coast.

F or over a decade the Tomcat was the 'tits' machine that every 'Joe Ace of the base' plumped for upon completion of his basic training. Fresh-faced jet jocks proudly wearing their newly-won wings of gold beat a well–trodden path to the fighter units at Miramar and Oceana. It was easy to see why the F-14 was such a desirable proposition at the time; no other aircraft in fleet service came close to matching the Grumman fighter's manoeuvrability, firepower or turn of speed.

Things began to change in the early 1980s, however, with the advent of the new A-7E Corsair II replacement, the McDonnell Douglas F/A-18A Hornet. Here was an aircraft possessing a thrust-to-weight ratio far superior to that of the F-14, which could deliver bombs with pinpoint accuracy and, most importantly from a pilot's

point of view, was a single-seater! The transistion of fleet attack squadrons from the A-7E to the F/A-18 has taken almost a decade to complete, but now the Navy of the 1990s has over 20 frontline Hornet units shared between 15 carrier air wings.

Mirroring the change in fleet air wing composition, the Navy Reserve was fortunate enough to receive Hornets far earlier than most pundits had anticipated. For decades the part–time Navy had had to make do with well-worn hand-me-downs from their frontline brethren, operating aircraft that were well past their prime and of no significant tactical use to anybody. Although the reservists' commitment was faultless, their ability to do the job was often adversely affected by their equipment.

Thanks to vigorous hawking in Washington DC in the

Devoid of all external stores bar a solitary centreline fuel tank, 'Lobo 413' cruises over the Pacific looking for a playmate. In this configuration the aircraft's legendary manoeuvrability and awesome thrust-to-weight ratio would make the Hornet difficult to beat in a head-to-head dogfight, particularly against an underpowered F-14A.

early 1980s by the then Secretary of the Navy John Lehman (a Navy reservist himself), these aircraft were finally replaced by current fleet types like the F-14A, updated E-2C, EA-6B and, perhaps most significantly, the F/A-18 Hornet. One of the first units to benefit from this new policy was the light attack squadron VA-305 'Lobos' at Point Mugu. Formed at NAS Los Alamitos, California, on 1 July 1970, the unit had initially been equipped with the venerable A-4C Skyhawk. A move to Point Mugu six months later coincided with the squadron's re-equipment with the more modern A-7A Corsair II. The Alpha model A-7s were traded in for newer Bravos in 1978, VA-305 trucking on with the antiquated Corsair IIs until January 1987.

The second light attack unit within Carrier Air Wing Reserve Thirty (CVWR-30), VA-305 followed sister-squadron VA-303's lead by trading in their A-7s for F/A-18s, redesignating as a fighter/attack (VFA) outfit in the process. As with the 'Golden Hawks' (who had received their first eight Hornets at NAS Lemoore, California, on 19 October 1985), the 'Lobos' were issued with second-hand F/A-18As which had previously served with VFA-125 'Rough Raiders', the Hornet training unit on the West Coast. Due to VFA-305's reserve status the squadron took 18 months to complete the transition onto the Hornet. However, since declaring itself operational in late 1988, the unit has participated in CVWR-30's carrier dets, NAS Fallon strike warfare deployments and numerous *Lobo Flag* exercises, all of which have proven the mettle of Navy reservists.

Heading inland towards Nevada and the strike warfare ranges at NAS Fallon, a pair of 'Lobos' keep their noses up to maintain station with the slower C-130 photo-ship. The aircraft in the foreground has only recently been assigned to the squadron's executive officer, with the nose and tail modex hastily doctored to reflect the Hornet's new 'owner'. The wingman wears only a two-digit fin modex; this style of designation is more common among Marine Corps Hornet operators. The blotchy and weatherbeaten appearance of 'Lobo 404' suggests that the Hornet is perhaps nearing a 1500- or 2000-hour deep strip-down maintenance period; the aircraft will be despatched to the Naval Air Rework Facility (NARF) at NAS North Island, where it will be rebuilt from the wheels up. Once the airframe has been reassembled and test flown, the Hornet will be resprayed and returned to VFA-305 for further use.

The Hornet is festooned with lumps and bumps, most of which have been grafted onto the airframes in post-factory modification programmes carried out over the years. The small wedges inboard of the navigation lights were retrofitted to all Hornets in the late 1980s in an effort to disturb the channelled airflow which washes over the leading edge extensions (LEXs) and violently buffets the twin fins, causing premature fatigue. Moving aft, the prominent fin root attachment lugs at the base of the vertical surfaces also appeared on most early Hornets after they had entered squadron service, McDonnell Douglas beefing up this weak point in the aircraft's structure following the appearance of stress cracks in many low-time F/A-18As.

CDR JACK MCGUIRE CO
WILD THANG

(Left) Former leader of the pack Cmdr. Jack 'Wild Thang' McGuire, crowned with a 'chocolate chip' desert combat helmet cover, performs his preflight checks before taxying out on yet another sortie. 'Wild Thang' led a six-Hornet VFA-305 det aboard the Navy's newest carrier, USS *Abraham Lincoln* (CVN–72), in September 1990 as the vessel undertook a two-month positioning cruise from Norfolk, Virginia, to its new home port at Alameda, California. Fulfilling the light strike duties for CVW-11, the 13 pilots and 156 maintenance crew exercised with both the Argentine and Chilean air forces during the carrier's Around-the-Horn voyage.

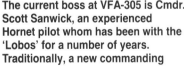

The current boss at VFA-305 is Cmdr. Scott Sanwick, an experienced Hornet pilot whom has been with the 'Lobos' for a number of years. Traditionally, a new commanding officer can expect to spend up to three years at the helm of a Navy squadron, having already served 18 months to two years as XO.

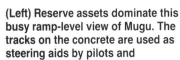
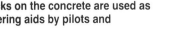

(Left) Reserve assets dominate this busy ramp-level view of Mugu. The tracks on the concrete are used as steering aids by pilots and groundcrews alike, these simple marks being accurately spaced so as to provide each aircraft with an adequate area in which to park.

When the sun disappears beneath the thick coastal fog that blankets Mugu, this specialised version of the Hornet will come into its element. Wearing the simple 'DT' codes of VMFA(AW)-242 'Bats', this night attack F/A-18D symbolizes the new breed of Hornet currently replacing the venerable A-6E Intruder in Marine Corps heavy attack squadron ranks. Equipped with a dedicated FLIR (Forward Looking Infrared), colour digital map displays and night vision goggles for the two-man crew, the F/A-18D is capable of performing precision strike missions 24 hours a day in virtually any weather. A total of seven squadrons are due to re-equip with the F/A-18D, allowing the weary A-6s to pass gracefully into retirement.

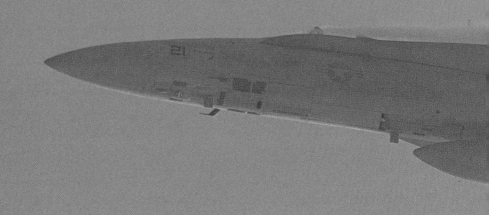

Aside from the VFA-305 F/A-18s, a dozen or so Hornets of various models can usually be found at Mugu undertaking trials work with VX-4 'Evaluators' and VX-5 'Vampires'. Both units were responsible for testing the aircraft's operational capabilities in the early 1980s prior to service release. VX-4 conducted the fighter portion of the Hornet's Initial Operational Test and Evaluation, the squadron being greatly impressed with the aircraft's high angle of attack (AOA) capability. Over a decade later, a new generation of 'Evaluators' still enjoy pushing the Hornet's AOA meter to the limit, streaming low pressure vortices over the aircraft's 'electric wing' in the process.

3: Maritime Patrol

(Previous page) Besides the Tomcats and Hornets that proliferate at Mugu, perhaps the most common Navy aircraft ranged up on the ramp is the elegant P-3 Orion. A full squadron of these potent maritime patrol sub-hunters are based here, their numbers being bolstered by a unique collection of specially modified Orions on strength with the PMTC. This particular P-3 (indulging in a thorough wash in the desalinization shower) looks just like any other Orion currently serving with the VP-fleet, except for the distinctive 'T'-shaped aerial on its spine. It is in fact one of a pair of Alpha–model Orions modified to carry the Sonobuoy Missile Impact Locating System (SMILS) within its roomy fuselage. Redesignated as EP-3As, the aircraft are flown by the PMTC in support of the Navy's submarine-launched ballistic missile test programme. The SMILS can determine the exact impact point of strategic re-entry bodies, rating the accuracy of the missile, and its trajectory.

Cleansed of the salt spray accumulated during the recently completed low-level mission, the EP-3A is parked up on the PMTC ramp once again. Behind it is the second SMILS EP-3A, while to its right is one of the three EP-3A EATS (Extended Area Test System) Orions on strength with the PMTC. These latter airframes have a large Raytheon Rotman lens phased array antenna mounted in a slab fairing that has been grafted onto the spine of the aircraft, just forward of the tail. Modified by Hayes International and Tracor at Mojave Airport in California, these weary airframes are used as airborne instrumentation stations in conjunction with missile testing performed over the Mugu ranges. Unlike their SMILS squadron mates, these Orions have been completely stripped of ASW equipment in order to make room for the radar consoles and associated computational equipment.

(Left) When you are preflighting an aircraft the size of an Orion, a ladder can come in very handy. Working from left to right, the flight engineer visually checks each of the Allison T56-A-14 turboprops and removes the intake debris covers. Once he has finished scaling the lofty heights the ladder is stored, along with the covers, in the squadron line shed and the engineer takes his place in the jump-seat between the pilot and co-pilot, both of whom have conducted their own walkaround checks.

(Right) Up at the sharp end things can get a little friendly prior to brakes off and rolling as the pilot, his number two and the engineer all endeavour to complete the seemingly endless series of instrument checks, and associated paperwork, and still maintain their launch slot time. Developed from Lockheed's stylish Electra propliner of the mid-1950s, the Orion reflects period instrumentation in its metal, rather than glass, cockpit environment. The single monitor that dominates the centre console provides the pilot with a real time tactical picture of the mission being fought by the sensor operators, buried between banks of displays and sonobuoy racks behind him in the aircraft's long fuselage.

The major Orion operator at the base is Reserve Patrol Squadron 65 (VP-65), nicknamed the 'Tridents'. Currently transitioning from the elderly P-3B TACNAVMOD (Tactical Navigation Modernization) version onto the more sophisticated Charlie model, the squadron is one of seven VP units assigned to the Commander Reserve Patrol Wing Pacific. VP-65 was commissioned on 1 November 1970 as part of a major reserve force reorganization, the unit pooling resources from four smaller patrol flights based at NAS Los Alamitos, California. Initially equipped with 12 SP-2H Neptunes, the 'Tridents' traded in their old Lockheeds for 'new' ones in the shape of the P-3 Orion in 1975. Over the next four years the squadron spent active duty periods in the western Pacific, serving on Guam and in the Philippines as the on-station VP squadron in support of Commando Task Force 72. Okinawa and Singapore featured in the unit's overseas det throughout the 1980s, as did Misawa in Japan, and Korat in Thailand.

(Right) Having completed a long sortie over the Pacific, a VP-65 crew return home to rest at Point Mugu. This underside view clearly shows the launch tube area, and the neat weapons bay immediately ahead of the wing: up to eight bombs, or a mix of torpedoes, aerial mines and Harpoon missiles can be housed in the generous weapons bay. Up to five weapons racks can also be fitted beneath each wing to increase further the Orion's hunter-killer capability.

Currently, VP-65 are trading in their old Orions for 'new' P-3Cs, freed from frontline units by the availability of more modern Update III aircraft. Externally, one of the major differences between the Bravo and Charlie models is the multi-tube sonobuoy launch area immediately aft of the wings, fitted as standard in the later version of the Orion. A total of 48 chutes can be utilized by the sensor team, the Orion carrying a mix of passive and active buoys which are primed and ready for use. The advantage of a multi-tube system is that the crew can lay down a rapid, solid pattern of buoys around a possible contact without having to worry about the reloading of tubes by hand from internal racks.

The P-3 fleet worldwide has always enjoyed a safety record second to none, thanks mainly to the aircraft's tried and tested Allison T56 turboprop powerplant. The original four-engine fit, as built into the Electra, was left virtually unmodified when Lockheed developed the P3V-1 as a replacement for the Neptune. Over the ensuing decades the T56 has remained essentially the same, the original A-10Ws, which produced 4500 shp, being progressively replaced with the current A-14 model, which is rated at 4910 shp. Crews often feather two engines while out on patrol to further extend the aircraft's range and loiter time on station. The still-born P-7A, which had been designed by Lockheed as the Orion's replacement, was to have been powered by the all-new 5150 shp General Electric GE38 turboprop. Future updates of the current Orion fleet may eventually see the P-3 equipped with this new engine.

4: Herks, Frogs and Drones

Missile testing is what Mugu is known for in the Navy, and one of the major organizations within the PMTC set-up crucial to the base's role is the Targets Directorate. Responsible for providing a variety of floating and flying targets for both aircraft and ships to fire at, the Directorate operates a varied fleet of types tasked with supporting everyday operations. Its largest assets are a pair of suitably gaudy DC-130A Hercules, heavily modified for drone-hauling missions. Seen here cruising out to its designated operational area deep inside the controlled missile range off the California coast, this aircraft is fully loaded up with four Ryan BQM-34S Firebee drones. Once the Hercules has reached its drop point the drone will be released from its underwing rack, and a controller on board the DC-130 will fire up the target's Teledyne J69-T-29 turbojet engine and commence flying the Firebee towards its contact.

Both the Firebee drone and its Hercules mothership were first used during the later years of the Vietnam War when the USAF experimented with unmanned reconnaissance vehicles over the combat zone. Under the auspices of the Multiple Drone Control Program, the ultimate Hercules mothership was developed when two HC-130H airframes were allocated for conversion, although the cessation of hostilities resulted in only a single DC-130H actually being built. Assigned to the 6514th Test Squadron at Eglin AFB, Florida, this solitary airframe was heavily used for test work, being able to carry four 10,000-lb drones, all of which could be simultaneously controlled from a special station mounted within the aircraft's capacious cargo bay. During the 1980s both the standard Hercules and the modified NC-130 were redesignated NC-130Hs, and are still used today in support of classified weapons testing.

Aside from the large BQM-34S, smaller drones like the supersonic BQM-34E/T and the basic BQM-74C can also be carried on the large underwing pylons of the DC-130A. The latter is ideal for simulating sea-skimming missiles, the controller aboard the Hercules guiding the small BQM-74 across the waves at naval vessels working up after refit, or undergoing post-commissioning shakedown tests. The drone can be programmed to emit active radar signals, or it can remain totally silent. Occasionally the ship's fire control team are allowed to launch a Standard surface-to-air missile at the drone, or engage the closing 'hostile' with a Phalanx gatling gun; but more often than not in these days of tight fiscal restraint, the drone is downed synthetically through computer simulation, splashed by its DC-130 controller and returned to Mugu by helicopter for overhaul and re-use.

The Hercules at Mugu are among the oldest C-130s still flying in regular service. Initially issued to the USAF in the late 1950s, the seven Hercules converted into drone directors wore the GC-130 designation until the mid-1960s. As part of the conversion, the traditional 'Pinocchio' radome containing the AN/APN-59 radar was removed and a larger, more pronounced 'thimble' nose grafted on in its place. Beneath the radome was a specialized AN/APN-49 tracking radar, which allowed the on-board controllers to fly the various drones. A microwave guidance system was also fitted just forward of the nose gear. Five DC-130As were transferred to the Navy in 1969 and allocated to Composite Squadron Three (VC-3). Eventually, the operation of the Herks was passed over to civilian contractors in the shape of Lockheed Aircraft Services, and Flight Systems Inc. The latter firm are currently responsible for operating the aircraft (still owned by the Navy) from their base at Mojave Airport.

Heading for a rendezvous with a hungry Tomcat out over the range, a Firebee uses a JATO (jet assisted take-off) rocket bottle to power away from the concrete launch pad at Mugu. Once exhausted, the booster will fall harmlessly away into the ocean and the drone's J69 engine will propel the target along at about 550 knots. Back at the PMTC, the drone's pilot flies the Firebee with the help of cockpit instruments and a computer. He watches the drone's progress towards the Tomcat on a large TV screen immediately above his console. The Tomcat is equipped with a Sparrow telemetry round which allows the crew to achieve lock-on and theoretical launch of the missile at the target without physically

destroying the $450,000 drone. The Firebee is not a sitting duck, however, as this particular drone has been fitted with an electronic jammer constructed specifically to render the F-14's AWG-9 radar useless. The Tomcat makes two close passes at the BQM-34, but on both occasions the crew fail to obtain a satisfactory radar lock-on. Carrying only 600 lbs of fuel, the Firebee's 20-minute endurance is rapidly coming to an end, so the controller calls 'Bingo!' over the intercom and breaks off the engagement.

(Right) The Firebee is directed back towards a designated recovery area where, as the fuel cuts out, the drone's nose pitches up, activating a drag chute which streams from the jettisoned tail cone pulling the main chute out with it. Once safely down in the water the Firebee broadcasts a strong location signal, which is homed in on by a CH-46 Sea Knight despatched from Mugu to pluck the drone from the Pacific. In position over the target, the helicopter crewman delicately leans out of the hovering CH-46 and lassoos the drone with a hook. Firmly attached to the central loading hoist, the BQM-34 is retrieved from its temporary swim and flown the short distance back to Mugu for overhaul.

The 'beehive' back at the Target Directorate is not a good place to nurse a hangover! Unmistakably marked in dayglo orange, the Firebees have been the staple missile target for the Navy for over 20 years. Large enough to simulate either a cruise missile or a small fighter, the BQM-34S can be tailored to suit virtually any threat requirement. Once returned to base following a test flight, the drone is broken down into components and thoroughly immersed in a freshwater bath to remove any salt build-up left over from its dunk in the Pacific.

The base Rescue Flight plays a key role in supporting operations from Mugu, their small fleet of venerable CH-46s being maintained in spotless condition by enthusiastic groundcrews. As with the drones, the Sea Knights are thoroughly hosed down back at base immediately after recovery. Unlike most other naval air stations, which rely on the SH-3D Sea King to perform any SAR work, Mugu needs a helicopter that can haul an underslung load, and the CH-46 easily copes with any base requirements.

Desert Storm combat veterans come in all shapes and sizes, but perhaps among the most unique are the US Marine Corps Remotely Piloted Vehicles (RPVs). Part of the 40-strong fleet that was sent to the Gulf, these RPVs provided battlefield commanders with real-time imagery of the combat zone 24 hours a day. Based with Pioneer units both ashore with expeditionary forces, and at sea aboard the battleships USS *Missouri* (BB 63) and USS *Wisconsin* (BB 64), the RPVs performed targeting missions for field artillery, Naval Gunfire (NGF) spotting for the vessels' awesome 16 in batteries, battle damage assessment, and general reconnaissance and surveillance work. Easy to maintain and capable of being fitted with all manner of sensor and optical equipment, the RPVs proved extremely effective in combat. In fact, towards the end of the war one RPV flew over a small group of Iraqi troops who, knowing the destruction that was to follow in its wake, quickly surrendered! The larger RPV in these photos actually bears the scars of an Iraqi bullet just below its control mast.

5: Missile Testing

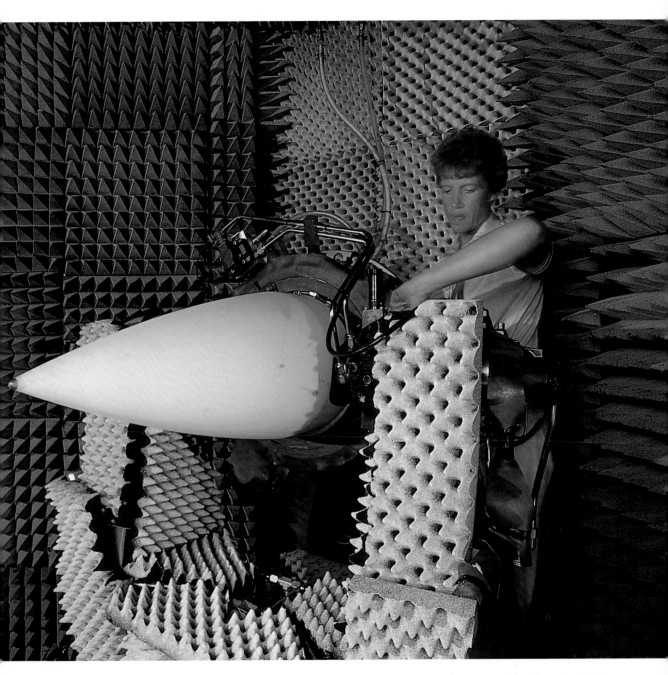

Although the PMTC's fleet of Tomcats, Hornets and Intruders perform the majority of the live missile testing out over the instrumented ranges, none of these weapons would ever get close to a fast jet were it not for the hours of bench testing performed in the many laboratories clustered within the confines of Point Mugu. Some of the most important work is carried out within this sinister-looking building, known as the radio frequency anechoic chamber. Here, a missile technician is securing an AIM-54C Phoenix sensor head to the test rack prior to energizing the radar. Totally echo-proof, the chamber is used to simulate target return signals and is capable of providing data indicative of actual flight conditions. Various wavelengths can be utilized, with sound, ultrasound, ultrasonic and microwave energy all available.

If you are a Tomcat pilot or RIO and you tend to be prone to airsickness, then this is the F-14 for you. Firmly mounted on a concrete pad, and enjoying charming ocean views, this Tomcat fuselage is actually utilized by the PMTC as the Systems Integration and Test Stations (SITS) laboratory for the F-14. Fully equipped with the latest fighter console displays, this mock fuselage even has a fully operable AWG-9 mounted up front, which scans the surrounding ocean through a rolladoor arrangement in the front of the building. Responsible for Software Support Activity (SSA) for the fleet's F-14s, the PMTC ensures that Tomcat crews receive missiles that interface totally with onboard systems in any environment. In a typical year technicians will spend up to 1,800 hours 'flying' the SITS, saving the Navy millions of dollars in jet fuel by eliminating all but the most crucial of test flights.

The Phoenix is the '.44 Magnum' of air-to-air missiles, capable of destroying a target at distances of up to 100 miles from the launch aircraft. Developed by the Hughes Corporation in the late 1960s specifically for the Navy, the AIM-54C has given the Tomcat community a virtually unrivalled ability to 'reach out and touch' the enemy way before he can return the gesture.

As is clearly visible in this view of an inert round being readied for the anechoic chamber, the Phoenix consists essentially of five separate sections. Working from left to right: the fibreglass radome covers the 'eyes' of the missile, the planar-array seeker head, which is in turn controlled by the weapon's brain, the miniaturized AN/DSQ-26B guidance radar. Within this section of the missile is an electrical battery, radar electronics unit and a transmitter/receiver. Immediately behind the guidance system is the 60 kg annular blast fragmentation warhead, which is triggered through a Downey Mk 334 proximity fuze or a Bendix infrared or direct action device. The missile's motor takes up most of the remaining space within the round, a long-burning Rocketdyne (Flexadyne) Mk 47 or Aerojet Mk 60 motor propelling the Phoenix at speeds of

up to Mach 5 over distances of 120 miles. Missing from this test round are the distinctive fins which guide the Phoenix through inputs from the autopilot, fitted in the tail of the missile. The rear fins are hydraulically driven and give the AIM-54 a continuous manoeuvrability throughout its interception profile. The latest version of the Phoenix, the AIM-54C, is a more robust missile which has a self–cooling capacity and is equipped with all-digital electronics, thus improving the weapon's reliability. A strapdown Nortronics inertial reference unit has improved the missile's accuracy, while rigorous testing by the PMTC has seen the AIM-54's electronic counter-counter measures capability increased and a new proximity fuse introduced.

Although not perhaps as high-tech as the previous cockpit layout, the 'shirtsleeves' office of the QF-86 Sabre drone at least has the pilot controlling an object that is airborne. With one hand gently pushing the throttle forward while the other steadily pulls the control column back, Cmdr. Bob Williams races down the 'blacktop' at 'San Nick', commencing yet another test sortie. Boss of the drone aircraft at the Target Directorate, Cmdr. Williams gets plenty of 'stick time' without having to leave his air-conditioned office.

Within the mock cockpit are all the essential flight controls and analogue dials, while in front of him three TV screens give him a God's eye-view through telemetry pods and computer graphics, of the drone aircraft's position in relation to the intercepting fighter or ship. The centre console relays real-time images from a small black and white TV camera mounted in front of the cockpit. All full–scale drones are based on San Nicholas Island, a small rocky outcrop 60 miles from Point Mugu, which is blessed with a 10,000-foot runway, $30 million worth of high-tech missile tracking and drone radio control equipment, and an abundance of wildlife.

There is a drone target available at Mugu to suit every possible mission profile that may need to be tested. Parked alongside the QF-86F Sabre is a QF-4N Phantom II, the other full-scale target utilized by the PMTC. Virtually all flying parameters encountered by today's fleet fighters can be reproduced between the two types. Opposing them are a selection of specialized drone targets. Clockwise from the Sabre they are: four different types of aerial tow target, including the TDU-34A (second in line), which can be towed behind an A-6, F-4 or A-4; the ubiquitous Ryan BQM-34S Firebee; an MQM-8G missile target, which is capable of achieving speeds up to Mach 2.8 and heights of 70,000 ft, as well as performing vertical dive attacks at up to 90° degrees on surface targets; a BQM-34T, which can achieve supersonic speeds and still manoeuvre at between three and five G; and finally a BQM-74C missile target, used essentially to test a ship's defences against sea-skimming missiles.

QF-86s are not cheap to maintain and operate, so relatively few are splashed on their very first mission. Aside from being fully converted for radio control, the drones are also wired up for telemetry shots from attacking fighters. A trio of antennae mounted on the aircraft's fin and wingtips record the theoretical interception for thorough analysis after the drone has recovered back at San Nicholas. Cannon shots can also be accurately measured without the Sabre taking physical hits. This particular aircraft is a veteran of four AIM-54 'interceptions'. QF-86Fs have been the staple target for Navy weapons tests for the last decade, and over 200 airframes have been shot down by a mix of missiles and guns. In order to maintain a suitably sized fleet for the PMTC programmes the Target Directorate has scoured the world looking for airworthy Sabres suitable for conversion. Currently the drone squadron consists mainly of ex-Japanese Air Self-Defense Force F-86Fs, most of which have only 1,300 to 1,500 flight hours on their airframes.

Firmly screwed into the side of the radio frequency control box, this red plug signifies that this QF-86 is now ready for flight by 'no live operator', abbreviated by PMTC crews who say that the drone is being piloted by Ensign Nolo. To enable the aircraft to fly safely without a man in the hot seat, technicians at the base fit a system of electromechanical servo controls to the Sabre's flying surfaces. If for some reason the pilots back at Mugu lose control of the aircraft due to a break in the radio link, the electronics fitted into the Sabre are programmed to guide the aircraft away from areas of population, maintaining a safe course until the drone runs cut of fuel.

Many of the drone controllers are ex-Navy fast jet pilots who have left the service to work as civilians within the PMTC organization. Among this crop of seasoned aircrew is Michael O. Jones, a former lieutenant-commander who now 'flies' both the QF-86F and the QF-4N. Before a prospective controller can sit down in his shirtsleeves and wrestle with the controls, he must first prove his proficiency on-type by taking the aircraft aloft for a series of check-rides. Once he has done this, the controller will remotely pilot a full-scale drone on a sortie out over the sea ranges; for this first flight a safety pilot will ride shotgun in the cockpit. As the number of suitable F-86s begins to dwindle, the Navy has turned to the F-4N for future drone requirements. First introduced in 1986, the QF-4N has proven a worthy opponent for fleet fighter crews; up to the middle of 1990, only six Phantom IIs had been downed during a total of 26 Nolo flights.

Control of the skies out over the Sea Test Range is crucial to both the safety and the efficiency of the PMTC. Boasting the largest test and evaluation facility in the Navy, Mugu's Pacific Ocean range comprises a fully instrumented 35,000 square mile area about 125 miles wide by 250 miles long. Range support facilities are co-ordinated from within this impressive computer centre, which controls precision tracking and surveillance radars, telemetry stations, control and display centres, communication networks, launch facilities, frequency monitors, safety and meteorological services, and data handling and processing. As can be seen on these glowing scopes, various 'enemy' targets can be threat-simulated out on the ranges in order to test systems fitted to both aircraft and ships.

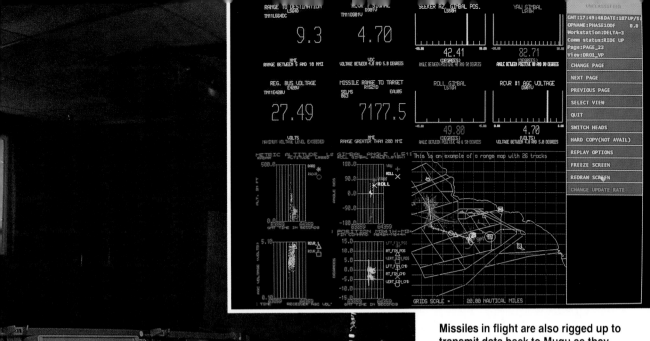

Missiles in flight are also rigged up to transmit data back to Mugu as they transit in towards their targets. All of this information can be generated synthetically through a telemetry shot at a drone target, thus providing the technicians back at base with the information they need at a fraction of the cost involved in loosing off the genuine article. The PMTC controls more than 30 separate laboratories, which are involved full-time in supporting developments in both missile and weapons system software technology. Special labs are currently working on both the Harpoon and AMRAAM systems, as well as electronic warfare in a brand new facility recently opened to deal exclusively with this special science.

(Left) This impressive bank of displays simulates a battle management centre that would be found buried within the superstructure of any flag-capable warship in the fleet. From here, prospective tactical commanders can hone their skills countering simulated threats with real warships and aircraft out on the range.

6: They Also Serve

Point Mugu seems to act as a magnet for role-specific 'specials' of well–known aircraft types, and an Antarctic-configured Hercules most definitely qualifies as role-specific. Assigned to VXE-6, this LC-130R spends six months each year on detachment at the squadron's forward operating station at Christchurch airport in New Zealand. Sent out every October to coincide with the Antarctic summer, the Hercules supports the operations of the National Science Foundation during 'Icebird' sorties to and from the various bases. All manner of goods are transported within the ski-equipped aircraft; these Hercules provide a vital air bridge for foodstuffs and technical equipment alike. Flying in arguably the world's worst climatic conditions, VXE-6 has suffered several losses since commencing operations in 1962.

Aside from the huge skis and the high-visibility paint scheme, the LC-130 is essentially the same as a standard Hercules. Both F- and R-models are utilized by VXE-6, these aircraft being maintained in Christchurch by Air New Zealand technical staff. The first Herks used in Antarctica were in fact USAF C-130Ds from the 61st Tactical Combat Squadron, then based at Sewart AFB in Tennessee. Under the leadership of Lt.Cmdr.Wilbert Turk, 12 Hercules were heavily utilized as 'trash haulers' throughout the summer of 1960. Suitably impressed by the Air Force's efforts, the Navy's Antarctic Station commander, Rear Admiral David M. Tyree, ordered the first LC-130Fs for use the following summer, soon after the 61st TCS had left for warmer climes.

Regular callers at Point Mugu are the twin-seat TA-7C Corsair IIs from the Naval Strike Warfare Center (NSWC) at Fallon. These aircraft are often used as a fast jet taxi service for ranking 'Strike U' officers, who

frequently head across to the PMTC for up-to-the-minute briefs on new weapons systems. The NSWC has a large fleet of aircraft available to staff for validating changes in the air wing training curriculum; experienced crews strap into Hornets, Intruders or Corsair IIs and head out over the ranges to put new attack profiles to the test.

Utilizing techniques learnt on the electronic warfare range at Fallon during periodic air wing dets, the crew of this EA-6B Prowler reaped havoc among Iraqi radar sites during the Gulf War. Armed with the deadly Texas Instruments AGM-88 HARM (High-speed Anti-radiation Missile), the Prowler crews successfully cleared the way for incoming strike packages en route to targets deep inside Iraq. As with all other frontline missiles currently in the Navy's arsenal, HARM was thoroughly tested over the ranges at Mugu.

Aside from the fighter types on strength with the PMTC, several 'mud-moving' A-6s also proudly wear the unique unit badge on their fins. This particular aircraft is configured in tanking mode, and is seen departing from the base in support of

No problem in checking the designation of this 'ramp-runner'; it looks very much like a 1987 Chevy Custom Deluxe four-door hard top, although we don't fancy the pilot's chances of getting it airborne before the catch fencing looms into sight!

the F-14D test programme. Unusually, the Intruder lacks the distinctive under-nose TRAM (Target Recognition and Attack Multisensor) turret present on virtually all operational A-6Es, which tends to suggest that this airframe is in fact a dedicated KA-6D tanker. However, the ventral refuelling receptacle is not visible either, hence the external centreline buddy-buddy pod. All in all, its current designation must be a matter of guesswork.

Dominating the base skyline is a massive stretch of rock, atop which sits the high-tech satellite equipment of the Laguna Peak tracking station. One in a chain of sites that forms the Navy Navigation Satellite System, the station tracks military satellites launched into a polar orbit from Vandenburg AFB. This vitally important system receives two-minute messages transmitted consecutively from the satellites as they orbit the Earth at an altitude of 600 nautical miles every 107 minutes.

The information stored in the satellite's data base for broadcasting back to Earth is continually updated by the ground network to ensure consistently accurate navigational readings. This information is sent out to over 80,000 vessels across the face of the globe, ballistic missile submarines and aircraft carriers being among the first users of this vital data when the system initially came on line in 1962.

7: Combat SAR

(Previous page) Having spotted a clearing in which to set down, the pilot commences his landing approach, guided in his descent by a watchful aircrewman perched in the doorway. HCS-5 (along with sister-squadron HCS-4 'Red Wolves' from NAS Norfolk, Virginia) was the first Naval Air Reserve unit to deploy to the Gulf. A pair of HH-60s and 50 active duty and selected reservists were loaded aboard an Air Force C-5 Galaxy on 11 December 1990 and flown to Tabuk airbase in the western Saudi desert, this location being chosen because of its proximity to the Iraqi border. Once declared operational, the HH-60 det provided around-the-clock strike rescue coverage for their sector, both HCS-4 and -5 personnel maintaining a measure of autonomy in order to achieve a self-sustained capability should the det be tasked to operate from two separate locations.

While on station in the Gulf the HCS-5 crews certainly appreciated the HH-60's immense reliability and endurance, the det flying more than 750 hours during the three-month deployment. The maintenance crews were able to achieve 90 per cent mission readiness for the helicopters, despite encountering extremely adverse conditions in the operational area. The talcum-fine sand particularly affected the helicopters' twin General Electric T700-401C turboshaft engines and the large rotor blades, causing premature weathering in both cases. The rotor blade pitch control bearings and blade dampeners were constantly replaced, as sand would work its way into the seals and eventually cause a massive seizure.

The youngest squadron to be found at Mugu is Helicopter Combat Support Special Squadron Five (HCS-5), appropriately equipped with one of the newest aircraft to enter Navy service. Established in October 1988, the 'Firehawks' received their first Sikorsky HH-60H Seahawks fresh from the factory in July 1989. Prior to equipping with the Seahawk the squadron had flown the HH-1K Huey as HAL-5, performing the mission of special warfare operations support with the Navy's crack SEAL teams.

Their new mounts have been specially developed for strike rescue sorties, the standard SH-60B LAMPS helicopter being stripped of its ASW systems and fitted out with mission-specific equipment. Some of the modifications include triple-redundant hydraulic and electrical systems, which allow the HH-60 to absorb considerable battle damage; a ballistics-tolerant drive train; sophisticated ECM systems including an APR-39 radar warning receiver, hover infrared suppressors and ALE-39 chaff and flare dispensers. As can be clearly seen in this photo, the HH-60 can also carry a pair of external 120 gal. fuel tanks to further increase its operational radius and loiter time on station.

HCS-5 regularly conduct aircrew training in and around the rugged, canyon-filled terrain that surrounds Point Mugu, as well as periodically detaching to Fallon to integrate strike rescue techniques into the deployed carrier air wing's pre-cruise work-up training. When at 'Strike U' the 'Firebirds' act as teachers, instructing the air wing's helicopter squadron in the latest rescue techniques. The HH-60 is the ultimate Navy rescue aircraft, capable of carrying two pilots and three crewmen 250 nautical miles at 145 knots, hover at heights up to 5,500 feet, and recover four downed aviators and return them safely to base. In its special operations role the Seahawk can carry an eight-man SEAL team, plus their equipment, 200 nautical miles to or from a specified drop zone. The helicopter can insert and extract SEALs by several means including fastrope, paradrop or rapelling; and the HH-60 is cleared to operate either at sea or on land, in any climate.

'Firebirds' crews have been rigorously trained in the use of ANVIS night vision goggles (NVGs), which allow the HH-60 to be flown at heights well under 100 feet in total darkness. Although the goggles do impede overall visibility (they have been compared to looking through two toilet paper rolls!), constant training with them has allowed all members of the crew to become fully proficient in their use. Gulf operations with NVGs proved even more demanding than back amongst the canyons at Mugu, as the desert was essentially featureless, which resulted in crews often flying a lot lower than they had estimated. Landing was also difficult, as sand kicked up by the rotor wash would totally envelop the helicopter and obliterate the horizon. Because of their role the HCS crews required pin-point navigation while in-theatre, so the HH-60s were quickly modified with a global positioning system (GPS) just prior to arrival in the Gulf. This move proved to be extremely fortuitous, as the featureless terrain of the desert made manual navigation a trying task. The crews also relied on the satellite communication equipment fitted in the USAF's strike rescue MH-60s and MH-53s.

High above the coastal sea fog, an HH-60H rattles along at close to full speed as it chases the C-130 photo-ship. To further decrease its infrared signature the HH-60 has special heat-absorbent baffles fitted to the engine exhausts; these devices cool emissions and channel them away from the helicopter itself. Plans are afoot to include two HH-60Hs within the traditional six-helicopter ASW squadrons embarked aboard the Navy's carriers. Although tasked primarily with the close-in ASW mission, these units also provide the plane-guard during cyclic ops, and would be charged with retrieving downed airmen in a war situation. This radical move has been made more cost-effective with the recent introduction of the SH-60F Ocean Hawk into air wing ranks, the commonality of the two helicopters easing the problems of introducing spares for a type hitherto foreign to a carrier deck.

(Below) Due to its role, the HH-60H is expected to come under fire from the enemy as it attempts to extract downed aircrew. No strike rescue would be attempted without air support from fighter and attack units, but the 'Firehawks' crews nevertheless wisely take no chances and mount a pair of 7.62 mm M60 machine guns on either side of the cabin. Future plans could see unguided rocket pods and air-to-surface TOW and Maverick missiles fitted to the helicopters. While sharp young eyes and reflexes are properly valued, this is not a regular member of the squadron.

8: Air Guard

The permanent Air Force presence at Mugu is maintained by a squadron of 16 C-130E Hercules transports of the 115th Tactical Airlift Squadron (TAS), California Air National Guard (ANG). Operating the most standard Herks on base, the 115th perform all manner of tasks both in support of other ANG units within the Republic, and farther afield with frontline assets during periods of active duty. The squadron has been in C-130s since April 1970, when it traded in its Boeing C-97C Stratofreighters for slightly secondhand Alpha model Hercules. However, most of these aircraft were sent to the Vietnamese Air Force in 1972 as part of the *Enhance Plus* programme, which saw the rapid transfer of military equipment to the region prior to the US withdrawal. The unit later received more Alphas and a few Bravos to bring the 115th back up to strength. The first Echoes arrived in 1975, and the squadron finally standardized on this type in 1980.

Cruising along at height, the Herk crew participate in some close 'follow my leader' formation work for the benefit of the camera. The unit has a long and distinguished history that stretches back to 16 June 1924, when the 115th Observation Squadron was activated at Clover Field, Santa Monica, and equipped with the Curtiss JNS-1 Jenny. Moving to Griffith Park, Los Angeles, immediately after formation, the 115th remained in the locale of the ever-growing city until called to active duty on 3 March 1941. At the time the squadron was flying the portly North American O-47, a type it continued to operate on submarine patrols up and down the California coastline until April 1943. Redesignated the 115th Liaison Squadron, the unit was issued with Stinson L-1s and L-5s and sent to Burma to help support the US Army in its fight against the Japanese. With the cessation of hostilities in August 1945 the squadron was deactivated, only to reform at Van Nuys Airport, California, just over 12 months later. Equipped with the B-26 Invader, the 115th was still flying the venerable Douglas twin five years later when called to active duty because of the Korean War.

Transferred to Langley AFB, Virginia, the 115th was assigned to the 47th Bombardment Group and re-equipped with the B-45A Tornado jet bomber. The squadron's flirtation with jet power ended in late 1951, however, as more B-26s were obtained and the unit was re-designated the 4430th Combat Crew Training Squadron. Returning to California in 1953, the weary Invaders were finally retired once and for all, only to be replaced by equally ancient F-51H Mustangs. The jet age definitively finally arrived for the 115th in January 1955 when the squadron picked up the first of its F-86A Sabres, becoming a tactical fighter squadron in the process. Things got a lot slower five years later when the C-97 loomed large on the horizon as a Sabre replacement; the unit became a tactical airlift squadron in the process, this designation still being carried today.

(Right) The cargomaster calls the shots as the pilot fires up the four Allison T56-A-7s one by one. As with the B-model, the Echo is fitted with four-bladed Hamilton Standard propellors. Although owned and operated by the 115th TAS, the unit is controlled by the 146th Tactical Airlift Wing (TAW), as denoted on the cheek of each Hercules.

(Right) When initially designed, the C-130E was viewed as a great improvement over the earlier Alpha and Bravo models, possessing a much longer range due to the 1360 US gal. pylon tanks mounted between the engines, and being able to lift 155,000 lbs of cargo (compared to 108,000 in the C-130A and 135,000 in the C-130B). To cope with the increased cargo capacity Lockheed strengthened the wing spars, beefed up the landing gear and thickened some of the skin panels. Externally, a small blister fairing containing an AN/APN-169A station-keeping device was affixed to the aircraft's spine just behind the cockpit. As with many other USAF, ANG and AFRES C-130Es, the 115th's aircraft have also been modified to fit a self-contained navigation system (SCNS), an enhanced derivative of the AN/APN-169A and an upgraded Adverse Weather Aerial Delivery System (AWADS).

As with all ANG and Navy Reserve units, the 115th benefits from being manned by highly experienced and motivated personnel. Doctors, lawyers, airline pilots or business executives for most of the year, these guys regularly exchange their civvies for a 'growbag' and take to the skies, performing a multitude of tasks in their Herks. Being only 40 miles north of Los Angeles at Mugu, the 115th has little trouble in recruiting new personnel into its ranks.

One of the specialized tasks undertaken by the 115th involves using the Hercules as a water-bomber in the summer months in an effort to control forest fires. The 115th convert several of their aircraft with a Modular Airborne Fire Fighting System (MAFFS) that enables the Hercules to drop 3000 US gallons of fire retardant in six to eight seconds over an area 150 ft wide by 2000 ft long. Developed by the FMC Corporation, the MAFFS can be rigged up inside a C-130 in less than two hours. The fire retardant, or water, is discharged through a pair of angled nozzles which hang over the lip of the rear cargo ramp. The fire season usually lasts from mid-May through to mid-October, and during that time two C-130Es and two MAFF-trained crews are maintained on standby to respond to calls. When configured with MAFF the C-130Es are stripped of their external tanks and pylons in order to reduce the aircraft's overall weight and increase its manoeuvrability over the drop zone.